PRINCEWILL LAGANG

The Billionaire Builder: Aliko Dangote's Journey to Africa's Richest

First published by PRINCEWILL LAGANG 2023

Copyright © 2023 by Princewill Lagang

All rights reserved. No part of this publication may be reproduced, stored or transmitted in any form or by any means, electronic, mechanical, photocopying, recording, scanning, or otherwise without written permission from the publisher. It is illegal to copy this book, post it to a website, or distribute it by any other means without permission.

Princewill Lagang asserts the moral right to be identified as the author of this work.

First edition

This book was professionally typeset on Reedsy.
Find out more at reedsy.com

Contents

1	The Billionaire Builder: Aliko Dangote's Journey to Africa's...	1
2	Building an Empire: Dangote's Cement Dominance	5
3	Dangote's Diversification: From Sugar to Salt, Flour, and...	8
4	Philanthropy and Impact: Aliko Dangote's Giving Back	11
5	Chapter 5	14
6	The Man Behind the Billions: Aliko Dangote's Personal...	17
7	A Vision Realized: Dangote's Impact on Africa's Economic...	20
8	The Road Ahead: Aliko Dangote's Vision for the Future	23
9	Lessons from the Billionaire Builder	26
10	Aliko Dangote's Enduring Legacy	29
11	A Bright Future: Aliko Dangote's Endless Impact	31
12	A Legacy of Transformation and Inspiration	34
13	Summary	37

1

The Billionaire Builder: Aliko Dangote's Journey to Africa's Richest

In a world where wealth and success are often measured by the size of one's bank account, few stories stand out as vividly as that of Aliko Dangote, Africa's richest man. His rise from a humble background to becoming a billionaire is a testament to the power of vision, determination, and unwavering perseverance. This chapter delves into the early life and formative experiences that set the stage for Aliko Dangote's extraordinary journey to becoming a global industrial magnate.

The Making of a Titan

Aliko Dangote's story begins in the dusty streets of Kano, Nigeria, on April 10, 1957. He was born into a business-oriented family, his grandfather having amassed wealth as a successful trader. This early exposure to entrepreneurship ignited the flames of ambition within the young Aliko. His parents, Mariya Sanusi Dantata and Mohammed Dangote, provided him with the love, support, and values that would shape his character.

As a child, Aliko displayed a remarkable sense of curiosity and an inherent ability to spot opportunities where others saw challenges. While many of his peers were content with the comfort of their daily routines, Aliko was keen to explore the world of commerce. At the tender age of eight, he would buy cartons of candy from his uncle's store and sell them to his classmates for a modest profit. This early entrepreneurial endeavor was a hint of things to come.

Aliko's father, Mohammed Dangote, recognized his son's potential and instilled in him the importance of discipline, hard work, and ethics. These values, deeply rooted in Aliko's upbringing, would serve as the cornerstone of his future success.

From Scholar to Entrepreneur

After completing his early education in Kano, Aliko ventured to the United States to pursue higher studies. He attended the prestigious Al-Azhar University in Cairo, Egypt, and later enrolled at Capital High School in Lagos, Nigeria. These experiences broadened his horizons and exposed him to diverse cultures and worldviews.

Upon returning to Nigeria, Aliko Dangote did not rest on the laurels of his education. He understood that true success would only come through practical application of his knowledge. In the late 1970s, he ventured into business, trading commodities such as rice, sugar, and cement. His innate business acumen, combined with the family's established connections, helped him navigate the complexities of Nigeria's emerging market.

Vision Takes Root

A turning point in Aliko Dangote's life came when he recognized the enormous potential in Nigeria's emerging cement industry. In 1979, he founded Dangote Group, a trading company that would later evolve into a multinational conglomerate. Aliko saw the dire need for infrastructure development in Nigeria and believed that by producing cement locally, he could help meet this demand.

However, the journey was far from smooth. The cement industry in Nigeria was dominated by foreign companies, and breaking their stranglehold was no easy task. Aliko faced fierce competition, bureaucratic red tape, and limited access to capital. But he persisted, leveraging his determination and unwavering commitment to his vision.

A Steady Climb to the Summit

Aliko Dangote's relentless pursuit of excellence led to the establishment of the Dangote Cement Factory in Obajana, Kogi State, Nigeria. This marked the beginning of his ascent to the summit of African industry. With state-of-the-art technology and a focus on cost efficiency, Dangote Cement rapidly became a powerhouse in the cement sector, providing jobs, fostering economic growth, and significantly reducing Nigeria's dependence on cement imports.

The years that followed saw Aliko Dangote diversify his business interests, venturing into sugar, salt, and flour production, among other industries. His visionary leadership and innovative thinking transformed the Dangote Group into one of Africa's largest and most successful conglomerates, covering a wide range of sectors, from agriculture to telecommunications.

A Beacon of Hope

As we close this chapter, it is evident that Aliko Dangote's journey from humble beginnings to becoming Africa's richest person is a story of audacious dreams, unwavering determination, and an unshakeable commitment to progress. His life is an inspiring narrative that showcases what is possible when vision meets resilience.

In the chapters that follow, we will delve deeper into the challenges and triumphs of Aliko Dangote's incredible journey. From his philanthropic efforts to his impact on the global business landscape, we will explore the man behind the billions, the billionaire builder, Aliko Dangote.

2

Building an Empire: Dangote's Cement Dominance

Aliko Dangote's journey to becoming Africa's richest man was marked by relentless ambition and unwavering determination. In this chapter, we dive into the pivotal role that the cement industry played in his ascent to economic prominence. Dangote's visionary leadership and innovative strategies transformed him from a budding entrepreneur to a global industrial titan.

The Cement Revolution

In the early 2000s, Aliko Dangote set his sights on a bold and ambitious mission: to revolutionize Nigeria's cement industry. At the time, Nigeria was heavily reliant on cement imports, making the country vulnerable to supply chain disruptions and currency fluctuations. Recognizing this vulnerability, Dangote saw an opportunity to not only secure Nigeria's cement supply but also to create a thriving domestic cement industry.

With characteristic determination, Aliko embarked on a massive infrastructure project, the construction of the Dangote Cement Factory in Obajana, Kogi State. This would be the largest cement production facility in Africa and a testament to his unwavering belief in the Nigerian market. The venture was not without its challenges, including navigating complex regulatory environments, securing funding, and tackling logistical hurdles, but Dangote persevered.

Pioneering Excellence

Dangote's approach to cement production was marked by a commitment to excellence. He invested heavily in cutting-edge technology and equipment, ensuring that his facilities were not only the largest but also the most advanced on the continent. This commitment to quality and efficiency allowed Dangote Cement to produce cement at a lower cost than its competitors.

Moreover, Dangote's emphasis on creating a vertically integrated business model allowed him to control every aspect of the supply chain, from limestone mining to distribution. This level of integration enabled Dangote Cement to maintain a competitive edge and significantly reduce its dependence on external suppliers.

A Game-Changing Industry Transformation

The impact of Aliko Dangote's cement venture was felt far beyond Nigeria's borders. It transformed the cement industry in Africa and demonstrated the potential for massive industrialization on the continent. His vision was a catalyst for other African countries to invest in their domestic cement production, reducing their reliance on imports.

The success of Dangote Cement resonated with investors, both domestic and international. The company went public on the Nigerian Stock Exchange in 2010, raising significant capital for further expansion. This marked a significant milestone in Dangote's journey, as it allowed him to finance even more ambitious projects.

From a Single Plant to a Global Network

The Obajana plant was only the beginning. Aliko Dangote's vision extended beyond Nigeria, and he began constructing cement plants in other African countries. Dangote Cement's reach expanded to countries like Senegal, Cameroon, Ethiopia, and South Africa, solidifying its status as a pan-African conglomerate. This global expansion was guided by Aliko's belief that African countries should be self-reliant and able to meet their own infrastructure demands.

Dangote Cement's exponential growth and success made Aliko Dangote a household name not just in Nigeria but across the African continent. His relentless pursuit of excellence, along with the creation of countless job opportunities, contributed significantly to local economies and infrastructural development in the countries where his plants operated.

The Billionaire Builder's Legacy

As we conclude this chapter, the reader is left with an understanding of how Aliko Dangote's foray into the cement industry was a pivotal chapter in his journey to becoming Africa's richest person. Dangote's unwavering commitment to excellence and self-reliance reshaped the cement industry in Africa and inspired countless entrepreneurs across the continent.

In the chapters that follow, we will explore the broader impact of Aliko Dangote's business empire, from his philanthropic endeavors to his role as a global industrial leader, and the lasting legacy he has created. The billionaire builder's story is a testament to the boundless possibilities of entrepreneurship and vision in the African context.

3

Dangote's Diversification: From Sugar to Salt, Flour, and Beyond

Aliko Dangote's journey to becoming Africa's richest individual is a tale of dynamic diversification. In this chapter, we explore how he expanded the Dangote Group into a diversified conglomerate with interests ranging from sugar to salt, flour, and various other industries. Dangote's visionary approach to business and his ability to identify opportunities in diverse sectors are key to understanding his unprecedented success.

Beyond Cement: Expanding the Empire

As the success of Dangote Cement continued to grow, Aliko Dangote recognized the importance of diversifying his business interests. He understood that relying solely on one industry could expose the Dangote Group to undue risk. With this foresight, he began to explore other sectors and industries where he saw potential for substantial growth.

The Sweet Success of Sugar

One of the early diversifications for Dangote was the sugar industry. Nigeria had a significant demand for sugar, and most of it was imported, making it a prime sector for investment. In 1999, Dangote Sugar Refinery was established, and it quickly became a leading player in the Nigerian sugar market.

Dangote's strategy in sugar production mirrored his approach to cement, focusing on large-scale production, vertical integration, and operational efficiency. His emphasis on quality and affordability made Dangote Sugar Refinery a household name in Nigeria.

Flourishing in the Flour Industry

With the sugar business thriving, Aliko Dangote set his sights on another industry with immense potential – flour milling. In 1999, Dangote Flour Mills was founded. The company soon became a significant player in Nigeria's flour market, producing a wide range of products used in the production of bread and other food items.

Dangote's commitment to quality and efficiency was once again evident in his approach to flour milling. His integration of the supply chain, from wheat importation to flour production and distribution, made Dangote Flour Mills a highly competitive force in the industry.

Salt of the Earth: Dangote Salt

Aliko Dangote's diversification extended even further to include the salt industry. In 2007, Dangote Salt was established. By leveraging his expertise in large-scale production and vertical integration, Dangote disrupted the salt market, offering high-quality, affordable salt to consumers.

Dangote's approach to the salt industry was not only driven by profit but also by a commitment to providing an essential product to the people of Nigeria. His philanthropic spirit was evident in the creation of the "Dangote Salt for

Life" initiative, aimed at addressing iodine deficiency disorders through the provision of iodized salt.

Diversification, Aliko Dangote's Way

Aliko Dangote's approach to diversification was underpinned by a set of key principles that had served him well in his earlier ventures. He emphasized the need for large-scale production, operational efficiency, and vertical integration. These principles allowed him to reduce costs, maintain quality control, and provide affordable products to consumers.

Dangote's diversification strategy was not limited to these sectors alone. The Dangote Group expanded into telecommunications, real estate, and the petrochemical industry, among others. His ability to identify promising sectors, develop a clear vision, and execute it with precision is a testament to his unparalleled business acumen.

A Visionary's Impact

As we conclude this chapter, it becomes evident that Aliko Dangote's diversification beyond cement was a pivotal step in his journey to becoming Africa's richest individual. His visionary leadership and ability to seize opportunities in a variety of industries transformed the Dangote Group into a truly diversified conglomerate.

In the chapters that follow, we will explore Aliko Dangote's philanthropic endeavors, his influence on the global business landscape, and the legacy he is leaving behind. The billionaire builder's story is not just one of business acumen but also of creating a lasting impact on the industries and people he serves.

4

Philanthropy and Impact: Aliko Dangote's Giving Back

Aliko Dangote's journey to becoming Africa's richest person is not solely about personal wealth and business success. In this chapter, we delve into the philanthropic endeavors that have defined his legacy and the impact he has made in addressing critical social and economic issues across the continent. Aliko Dangote is not only a billionaire builder but also a committed philanthropist.

A Heart for Giving: Dangote Foundation

Aliko Dangote's philanthropic journey began with the establishment of the Dangote Foundation in 1994. The foundation's mission was clear: to improve the well-being of people in Nigeria and across Africa. Aliko's commitment to philanthropy was deeply rooted in his belief that, as his wealth grew, so did his responsibility to give back to the less fortunate.

The Dangote Foundation focused on a wide range of initiatives, including health, education, and poverty alleviation. Aliko's belief in the transformative power of education led to scholarships for underprivileged students, the construction of schools, and the provision of educational materials.

Fighting Disease: Dangote's Contribution to Health

One of the most significant contributions of the Dangote Foundation was in the fight against diseases, particularly the battle against polio. Nigeria was one of the last countries to remain polio-endemic, and Aliko Dangote recognized the urgent need to address this public health crisis.

The Dangote Foundation joined forces with global health organizations and government agencies, contributing substantial financial resources and expertise to support polio eradication efforts. Thanks to this commitment, Nigeria was declared polio-free in 2020, a significant milestone in the fight against the disease.

Aid in Times of Crisis

Aliko Dangote's philanthropic spirit extended to disaster relief efforts. Whether it was natural disasters or humanitarian crises, the Dangote Foundation stepped in to provide aid and relief to affected communities. Dangote's quick response to such events showcased his dedication to helping those in need, even in the most challenging circumstances.

Beyond Nigeria: Pan-African Impact

Aliko Dangote's philanthropic efforts extended beyond the borders of Nigeria, reflecting his commitment to the well-being of the entire African continent. The Dangote Foundation initiated projects in several African countries, including Ghana, Niger, and Cameroon. These projects encompassed a wide range of initiatives, from healthcare to poverty reduction and education.

A Vision for a Better Africa

Aliko Dangote's philanthropy is not just about providing short-term relief but also about creating sustainable change. His vision for a better Africa includes initiatives aimed at economic empowerment, agricultural development, and job creation. By focusing on the long-term impact of his giving, Dangote has sought to uplift entire communities and, in turn, stimulate economic growth.

A Philanthropic Legacy

As we conclude this chapter, it is clear that Aliko Dangote's philanthropy is a fundamental part of his identity and legacy. His giving has touched the lives of countless people and has had a profound impact on public health, education, and disaster relief efforts across the African continent.

In the chapters that follow, we will explore Aliko Dangote's influence on the global business landscape, his visionary leadership, and the lasting legacy he is creating for generations to come. The billionaire builder's story is not just one of business acumen but also of compassion and commitment to making the world a better place.

5

Chapter 5

Chapter 5: A Global Industrial Titan: Aliko Dangote's Influence

Aliko Dangote's journey from a modest beginning to becoming Africa's richest person has left an indelible mark on the global business landscape. In this chapter, we explore his influence as a global industrial titan, the impact of the Dangote Group on various industries, and his vision for the future.

A Global Conglomerate

Aliko Dangote's remarkable journey has transformed the Dangote Group into a global conglomerate with interests spanning several industries, including cement, sugar, salt, flour, telecommunications, and more. His commitment to excellence, operational efficiency, and continuous expansion has made the Dangote Group a force to be reckoned with in the international business community.

Driving Economic Growth

Dangote's contributions to the economies of the countries in which he operates are profound. His massive industrial projects have generated thousands of jobs, fostering economic growth and development. The Dangote Group's focus on local production has not only reduced the reliance on imports but has also improved self-sufficiency and created value chains that extend beyond the borders of Nigeria.

African Industrialization

Aliko Dangote is an advocate for industrialization in Africa. He believes that African nations should be self-reliant and able to meet their own infrastructure and manufacturing needs. His investments in diverse sectors and commitment to local production serve as a model for African nations seeking to reduce their dependence on foreign goods and services.

International Partnerships

Dangote's influence extends beyond Africa's shores. He has forged strategic partnerships with international corporations and governments, contributing to the global reach of the Dangote Group. These collaborations have allowed the conglomerate to tap into global resources and expertise while simultaneously expanding Africa's footprint in the international business community.

A Vision for the Future

Aliko Dangote's vision extends beyond the present day. He has set ambitious goals for the Dangote Group, which include further diversification and expansion into new industries and markets. His commitment to innovation and excellence continues to drive the conglomerate's growth and influence.

Inspiring the Next Generation

Aliko Dangote's journey serves as an inspiration to entrepreneurs and business leaders in Africa and around the world. His story demonstrates that with vision, determination, and hard work, it is possible to create a global business empire and make a lasting impact on society.

A Lasting Legacy

As we conclude this chapter, it is clear that Aliko Dangote's influence as a global industrial titan is not limited to his wealth but extends to the industries he has transformed, the economies he has supported, and the inspiration he has provided to future generations of business leaders.

In the chapters that follow, we will delve deeper into the life and legacy of Aliko Dangote, exploring the man behind the billions, the billionaire builder, and the enduring impact he is creating in Africa and beyond.

6

The Man Behind the Billions: Aliko Dangote's Personal Journey

Aliko Dangote's life and success are not only defined by his wealth and business ventures but also by his personal journey, values, and the qualities that have shaped him into the iconic figure he is today. In this chapter, we take a closer look at the man behind the billions, exploring his character, principles, and the experiences that have molded him.

A Relentless Work Ethic

Aliko Dangote's remarkable journey to becoming Africa's richest individual is a testament to his unwavering work ethic. From his early entrepreneurial ventures as a child to his transformation of the Dangote Group into a multinational conglomerate, Dangote has consistently shown dedication and a willingness to put in the effort required for success.

The Power of Vision

Vision has been a driving force in Aliko Dangote's life. He possesses a unique ability to see opportunities where others might see challenges. His vision for Africa's industrialization and economic self-sufficiency has guided his business ventures and philanthropic efforts.

Leadership and Innovation

Dangote is not only a businessman but also a leader and innovator. He has displayed the ability to identify and implement groundbreaking strategies in various industries, from cement to sugar and salt. His emphasis on vertical integration and cost efficiency has set the benchmark for operational excellence.

Values and Ethics

Aliko Dangote's upbringing and family values have played a crucial role in shaping his character. His father instilled in him the importance of discipline, hard work, and ethics. These values are evident in his business practices, as he has consistently operated with integrity and respect for the communities in which he works.

A Philanthropic Spirit

Beyond business success, Dangote's philanthropic endeavors showcase his compassion and commitment to giving back. His efforts in education, healthcare, and disaster relief have touched countless lives. Dangote's belief in using his wealth to make a positive impact on society is a core part of his identity.

Challenges and Resilience

Aliko Dangote's journey has not been without its share of challenges. He faced formidable obstacles in various industries, from regulatory hurdles to fierce competition. However, his resilience and determination enabled him to overcome these challenges and achieve unprecedented success.

A Visionary for Africa's Future

Aliko Dangote's influence extends beyond his business empire. He is a visionary leader who advocates for the industrialization of Africa and self-sufficiency. His success story serves as a source of inspiration and a blueprint for future generations of entrepreneurs in Africa and around the world.

A Billionaire Builder's Legacy

As we conclude this chapter, we gain a deeper understanding of the man behind the billions, Aliko Dangote. His life is not only a tale of business acumen and success but also a story of vision, hard work, and philanthropy. Aliko Dangote's legacy is one that will continue to shape the business landscape in Africa and inspire those who aspire to create lasting impact in their communities and beyond.

7

A Vision Realized: Dangote's Impact on Africa's Economic Landscape

Aliko Dangote's influence is not limited to his own success or the industries he has transformed. It extends to the broader economic landscape of Africa. In this chapter, we explore how Dangote's vision and initiatives have reshaped the continent's economic outlook and his role as a driving force behind Africa's growth.

Industrialization and Self-Reliance

Aliko Dangote's unwavering commitment to industrialization and self-reliance in Africa has had a profound impact on the continent. His ventures in sectors like cement, sugar, salt, and flour have demonstrated that Africa can produce goods of international quality and meet its infrastructure and consumption needs without heavy reliance on imports.

Job Creation and Economic Growth

Dangote's investments have been instrumental in job creation and economic growth in African countries. His massive industrial projects have generated thousands of jobs directly and indirectly, contributing to poverty reduction and improved living standards for countless individuals and families.

Reduction of Import Dependency

Before Dangote's foray into various industries, many African countries were heavily reliant on imports for essential goods. Dangote's emphasis on local production and vertical integration has helped reduce this dependence and improve self-sufficiency.

Inspiration for Entrepreneurs

Aliko Dangote's journey from humble beginnings to becoming Africa's richest person is a source of inspiration for countless entrepreneurs across the continent. His success story demonstrates that with vision, determination, and hard work, Africans can build thriving businesses and contribute to the continent's growth.

Global Competitiveness

Dangote's commitment to operational excellence and cost efficiency has not only made his businesses competitive on a regional scale but also on a global one. His focus on innovation and quality has enabled his companies to compete with international giants, bringing global recognition to African industries.

Investor Confidence in Africa

Dangote's success and the growth of the Dangote Group have inspired investor confidence in Africa. His ability to attract investments, both domestic and international, has bolstered the perception of Africa as a viable destination for business opportunities and economic growth.

A Role Model for Philanthropy

Aliko Dangote's philanthropic efforts have set a standard for other successful individuals and corporations. His contributions to healthcare, education, and disaster relief efforts have shown that philanthropy can be a powerful tool for positive change, not only in Africa but around the world.

A Shaper of Africa's Future

As we conclude this chapter, it becomes evident that Aliko Dangote's impact on Africa's economic landscape is not limited to his own businesses. His vision, leadership, and unwavering commitment to the continent's growth have positioned him as a pivotal figure in shaping Africa's economic future.

In the chapters that follow, we will delve deeper into the man behind the billions, Aliko Dangote, and the lasting legacy he is creating for generations to come. The billionaire builder's story is not just one of personal success but also of transforming Africa's economic landscape and inspiring positive change.

8

The Road Ahead: Aliko Dangote's Vision for the Future

Aliko Dangote's journey to becoming Africa's richest person is marked not only by his past achievements but also by his vision for the future. In this chapter, we explore his ongoing and upcoming endeavors, as well as the legacy he intends to leave for generations to come.

Continued Diversification

Aliko Dangote's vision extends to further diversification of the Dangote Group. He aims to explore new industries and sectors that align with his commitment to industrialization and self-reliance in Africa. By expanding into diverse fields, he seeks to contribute to the economic development of the continent.

Agricultural Revolution

One of Dangote's key focus areas is the agricultural sector. He recognizes the potential for agriculture to drive economic growth and create employment opportunities across Africa. With initiatives such as rice and tomato production, Dangote aims to revolutionize the agricultural landscape, reduce food imports, and stimulate rural development.

Infrastructural Development

Dangote's investments in infrastructure are geared towards enhancing Africa's transportation and logistics networks. His ambitious plans for building a world-class petroleum refinery and a fertilizer plant in Nigeria are not only business ventures but also contributions to Africa's infrastructure development.

Education and Skills Development

Dangote's commitment to education remains strong. He believes that quality education is key to building a skilled and productive workforce. His scholarship programs and support for educational institutions continue to provide opportunities for young Africans to receive quality education.

Technology and Innovation

In an ever-evolving global landscape, Dangote recognizes the importance of technology and innovation. He is poised to invest in research and development to drive technological advancements in various sectors, making African industries more competitive on the world stage.

Global Influence and Partnerships

Dangote's global influence is set to expand further through strategic partnerships with international corporations and governments. These collaborations will not only facilitate the growth of the Dangote Group but also bring African businesses and industries to the forefront of the global economy.

Sustainable Development and Philanthropy

Sustainability is a core component of Dangote's vision. He aims to ensure that the growth of his businesses aligns with environmental and social responsibility. His philanthropic efforts will continue to focus on critical issues like health, education, and disaster relief.

Inspiration for the Next Generation

As he looks ahead, Dangote is keen to inspire the next generation of African entrepreneurs. His story is a testament to the potential that exists within the continent, and he aims to serve as a role model for those who aspire to create positive change through business and philanthropy.

A Lasting Legacy

Aliko Dangote's vision for the future is not just about building a prosperous business empire but also about leaving a lasting legacy that will shape Africa's economic landscape for generations to come. His impact goes beyond wealth; it is about making a difference in the lives of people and the development of the continent.

Conclusion

As we conclude this chapter, it is evident that Aliko Dangote's journey is far from over. His vision for Africa's growth and self-reliance continues to drive him to new heights, and his influence in various sectors remains profound. The man behind the billions is not resting on his laurels but is actively shaping a brighter future for Africa and its people.

9

Lessons from the Billionaire Builder

Aliko Dangote's journey from humble beginnings to becoming Africa's richest individual is rich with lessons and insights that can inspire and guide individuals in their own pursuits. In this chapter, we distill key lessons from Dangote's life and achievements, offering valuable takeaways for aspiring entrepreneurs and business leaders.

Lesson 1: Vision and Purpose

Aliko Dangote's story underscores the power of having a clear vision and purpose. His unwavering commitment to industrialization and self-reliance in Africa has been the driving force behind his ventures. The lesson is clear: define your vision and let it guide your actions.

Lesson 2: Perseverance and Resilience

Dangote's journey was marked by numerous challenges and setbacks, but his perseverance and resilience carried him through. He teaches us that adversity is part of the journey, and success often comes to those who can weather the storm and keep pushing forward.

Lesson 3: Hard Work and Dedication

Dangote's relentless work ethic and dedication to his ventures are evident in his success. The lesson here is that success is rarely handed to anyone; it is earned through hard work, commitment, and a willingness to put in the effort required.

Lesson 4: Continuous Learning

Dangote's education and international experiences broadened his horizons and exposed him to new ideas and opportunities. Lifelong learning is a key takeaway—never stop seeking knowledge and expanding your horizons.

Lesson 5: Ethics and Integrity

Dangote's commitment to ethics and integrity in his business practices is a crucial lesson. Building a reputation for honesty and fair dealing is not only morally right but also good for long-term success.

Lesson 6: Embrace Diversification

Dangote's diversification into multiple industries showcases the value of exploring diverse opportunities. The lesson here is to not limit your ambitions but be open to exploring new sectors and markets.

Lesson 7: Impact Through Philanthropy

Dangote's philanthropic efforts serve as a reminder that success is not just about personal wealth but also about the positive impact one can make on society. Giving back and helping others is a noble pursuit that can bring fulfillment and leave a lasting legacy.

Lesson 8: Inspire and Mentor Others

Aliko Dangote's journey is a source of inspiration for aspiring entrepreneurs. The lesson here is to not only achieve personal success but also to pay it forward by inspiring and mentoring the next generation of business leaders.

Lesson 9: Think Globally

Dangote's global outlook and international partnerships highlight the importance of thinking globally, even while building a business locally. The lesson is to recognize that the world is interconnected, and opportunities can be found beyond one's borders.

Lesson 10: Create a Lasting Legacy

Dangote's vision for the future is about creating a legacy that will impact future generations. The lesson here is that true success goes beyond personal gain; it is about making a meaningful and lasting difference in the world.

Conclusion

Aliko Dangote's journey is a remarkable testament to what can be achieved with vision, hard work, integrity, and a commitment to making a positive impact. These lessons from the billionaire builder offer a roadmap for those who aspire to not only achieve personal success but also to contribute to the betterment of society and the world at large.

10

Aliko Dangote's Enduring Legacy

As we conclude our journey through the life and accomplishments of Aliko Dangote, we reflect on the enduring legacy of the billionaire builder. In this final chapter, we explore the lasting impact he has had on Africa and the world, as well as the inspiration and hope he leaves for generations to come.

A Legacy of Economic Transformation

Aliko Dangote's legacy is undeniably one of economic transformation. His vision for industrialization and self-reliance in Africa has not only been realized through his businesses but has also inspired others to follow in his footsteps. He has shown that Africa can produce goods of international quality and meet its infrastructure and consumption needs.

A Champion of Philanthropy

Dangote's legacy extends to his philanthropic efforts. The positive change he has made in healthcare, education, and disaster relief is a testament to his commitment to improving the lives of people across Africa. He leaves behind a legacy that shows the immense impact philanthropy can have on society.

Inspiration for Future Generations

Aliko Dangote's journey is an enduring source of inspiration for aspiring entrepreneurs and business leaders in Africa and beyond. His success story demonstrates that with vision, determination, and hard work, individuals can build thriving businesses and create positive change in their communities and the world.

A Vision Realized

Dangote's legacy is one of a vision realized. His unwavering commitment to industrialization and self-reliance in Africa has reshaped the continent's economic landscape. The impact of his ventures, from cement to sugar, salt, and flour, is felt across Africa, and his global influence is a testament to his success.

A Lasting Influence

As we close the final chapter of this narrative, we are left with the knowledge that Aliko Dangote's influence is far from ephemeral. His legacy as a global industrial titan, philanthropist, and visionary leader will continue to shape the future of Africa and inspire those who aspire to follow in his footsteps.

Aliko Dangote, the billionaire builder, has created a legacy that reaches beyond wealth and business. His life serves as a beacon of hope and a testament to the boundless possibilities of entrepreneurship, vision, and perseverance. His impact on Africa and the world will endure, reminding us that the journey from humble beginnings to extraordinary success is a path that can be walked by those who dare to dream and work tirelessly to realize their vision.

11

A Bright Future: Aliko Dangote's Endless Impact

As we conclude this book on the life and legacy of Aliko Dangote, we peer into the horizon and imagine the enduring impact of the billionaire builder. This final chapter envisions the ongoing influence of Aliko Dangote and the ever-evolving legacy he leaves for Africa, its people, and the global business community.

A Vision Carried Forward

Aliko Dangote's vision for Africa's industrialization and self-sufficiency will continue to be carried forward by the Dangote Group and future leaders. The principles and values he instilled in his businesses, such as operational excellence and ethical practices, will remain integral to the conglomerate's success.

The Next Generation

Dangote's influence as a mentor and role model will extend to the next generation of African entrepreneurs. His story will inspire them to dream big, work hard, and make a difference in their communities and beyond.

Economic Transformation

Dangote's impact on Africa's economic transformation will persist and expand. As the Dangote Group continues to diversify and invest in various sectors, it will contribute to job creation, self-reliance, and poverty reduction across the continent.

Global Partnerships

The international partnerships forged by Aliko Dangote will remain a cornerstone of the Dangote Group's global influence. These collaborations will bring African industries to the forefront of the global economy, showcasing the continent's potential.

Innovations and Sustainability

The Dangote Group's commitment to innovation and sustainability will endure. As new industries and technologies emerge, the conglomerate will continue to lead the way in operational excellence, reducing environmental impact, and maintaining quality standards.

Philanthropic Impact

Dangote's philanthropic spirit will remain a beacon of hope for those in need. The Dangote Foundation's initiatives in education, healthcare, and disaster relief will continue to provide vital support to communities across Africa.

Inspiration and Legacy

Aliko Dangote's life story and legacy will serve as a timeless source of inspiration for generations to come. His remarkable journey will remind individuals that they too can overcome challenges, build successful businesses, and make a lasting impact.

Conclusion

In closing this book, we envision a bright future influenced by the enduring impact of Aliko Dangote. His vision, values, and accomplishments will continue to shape Africa's economic landscape, inspire the next generation of leaders, and offer hope for a brighter and more self-reliant future. Aliko Dangote's story is a testament to the limitless possibilities of entrepreneurship, determination, and the power of making a positive difference in the world.

12

A Legacy of Transformation and Inspiration

As we come to the end of this book, we reflect on the enduring legacy of Aliko Dangote, the billionaire builder, and the impact he has had on Africa and the world. This final chapter encapsulates the overarching themes and lessons from his life and career.

Legacy of Transformation

Aliko Dangote's legacy is one of transformation. His unwavering vision for industrialization and self-reliance in Africa has reshaped the economic landscape of the continent. Through diversification, innovation, and philanthropy, he has not only built a business empire but has also catalyzed economic growth, job creation, and self-sufficiency.

Leadership and Vision

Dangote's life exemplifies the power of visionary leadership. His ability to see opportunities where others see challenges and to stay committed to his vision has been instrumental in his success. His life teaches us that leadership is not just about reaching the pinnacle of success but about inspiring others to dream big and work tirelessly.

Perseverance and Resilience

A key lesson from Dangote's journey is the importance of perseverance and resilience. He faced innumerable obstacles and setbacks, but he never wavered. His story reminds us that determination and grit are crucial on the path to success.

Ethics and Integrity

Dangote's commitment to ethical business practices is a reminder that success should never come at the expense of integrity. Building a reputation for honesty and fair dealing is not just a moral choice but a key to long-term success.

Global Impact

Aliko Dangote's influence extends far beyond Africa's borders. His strategic partnerships and international collaborations have not only brought global recognition to African industries but have also solidified Africa's position in the global business community.

Philanthropic Spirit

Dangote's philanthropic endeavors have set a standard for those who have the means to give back. His contributions to healthcare, education, and disaster relief have shown that philanthropy can be a powerful tool for positive change, both in Africa and around the world.

Inspiration for Generations

One of the most enduring aspects of Aliko Dangote's legacy is the inspiration he provides for future generations. His story is a testament to what can be achieved with vision, hard work, and a commitment to making a positive impact. He leaves behind a blueprint for aspiring entrepreneurs and business leaders.

A Legacy Continues

As we conclude this book, we recognize that Aliko Dangote's legacy is far from finite. His impact will continue to shape Africa's economic landscape and inspire those who seek to make a difference. Aliko Dangote, the billionaire builder, is not just a figure of the past but a beacon of hope for the future, a symbol of what can be achieved with dedication, ethics, and the drive to create a lasting impact.

13

Summary

In this comprehensive book, we've delved into the remarkable life and legacy of Aliko Dangote, Africa's richest individual and a true visionary leader. Here is a summary of the key chapters and themes explored throughout the book:

Chapter 1: The book begins by introducing Aliko Dangote, a self-made billionaire from Nigeria, and his rise to become Africa's richest person. We explore his early life, family background, and the values instilled in him by his parents.

Chapter 2: This chapter delves into the early entrepreneurial ventures that shaped Dangote's business acumen. His ventures in commodities and trading laid the foundation for his future success.

Chapter 3: Dangote's journey takes a significant turn as he enters the cement industry, establishing Dangote Cement, which becomes the cornerstone of his wealth and success.

Chapter 4: Dangote's story goes beyond business success; it encompasses his philanthropic efforts through the Dangote Foundation. We explore his contributions to healthcare, education, and disaster relief, showcasing his compassion and commitment to giving back.

Chapter 5: Dangote's influence expands to global proportions as he diversifies the Dangote Group into various industries beyond cement. We delve into his impact on sectors like sugar, salt, flour, and telecommunications.

Chapter 6: This chapter paints a picture of Dangote as a global industrial titan, reshaping the economic landscape of Africa and advocating for industrialization and self-reliance.

Chapter 7: Dangote's vision for the future includes further diversification, agricultural development, and a focus on technology and innovation. We explore his commitment to a sustainable and self-sufficient Africa.

Chapter 8: Aliko Dangote's legacy extends beyond his wealth and businesses. His philanthropic efforts, ethical practices, and commitment to excellence serve as lessons for future generations of entrepreneurs and leaders.

Chapter 9: The enduring impact of Aliko Dangote is envisioned, highlighting the perpetuation of his vision, the inspiration he provides, and his contributions to economic transformation.

Chapter 10: This chapter encapsulates the overarching themes and lessons from Aliko Dangote's life and career, emphasizing his legacy of transformation, leadership, perseverance, ethics, global impact, philanthropy, and inspiration.

Chapter 11: As we peer into the future, we imagine the ongoing influence of Aliko Dangote and the ever-evolving legacy he leaves for Africa, its people, and the global business community.

Chapter 12: This final chapter summarizes the enduring legacy of Aliko Dangote, emphasizing his impact as a visionary leader, the inspiration

SUMMARY

he provides for future generations, and the lessons he imparts on ethics, perseverance, and global influence.

Aliko Dangote's journey is a testament to what can be achieved with vision, hard work, ethics, and a commitment to making a positive impact. His life story serves as a source of inspiration for individuals aspiring to build successful businesses and create lasting change in their communities and the world.

www.ingramcontent.com/pod-product-compliance
Lightning Source LLC
LaVergne TN
LVHW010439070526
838199LV00066B/6097